The **Rio Grande**

by Kathleen Fahey

Gareth Stevens Publishing
A WORLD ALMANAC EDUCATION GROUP COMPANY

Please visit our web site at: www.garethstevens.com
For a free color catalog describing Gareth Stevens Publishing's list of high-quality
books and multimedia programs, call 1-800-542-2595 (USA) or 1-800-387-3178
(Canada). Gareth Stevens Publishing's fax: (414) 332-3567.

Library of Congress Cataloging-in-Publication Data

Fahey, Kathleen.
    The Rio Grande / by Kathy Fahey.
       p. cm. — (Rivers of North America)
    Includes bibliographical references and index.
    Contents: The big river—From source to mouth—The life of the river—River of villages—
A vital source—Places to visit—How rivers form.
    ISBN 0-8368-3760-6 (lib. bdg.)
    1. Rio Grande—Juvenile literature. [1. Rio Grande.] I. Title. II. Series.
  F392.R5F345   2003
  976.4'4—dc21   2003042739

This North American edition first published in 2004 by
Gareth Stevens Publishing
A World Almanac Education Group Company
330 West Olive Street, Suite 100
Milwaukee, Wisconsin 53212 USA

Original copyright © 2004 The Brown Reference Group plc. This U.S. edition copyright © 2004
by Gareth Stevens, Inc.

Author: Kathy Fahey
Editor: Tom Jackson
Consultant: Judy Wheatley Maben, Education Director, Water Education Foundation
Designer: Steve Wilson
Cartographer: Mark Walker
Picture Researcher: Clare Newman
Indexer: Kay Ollerenshaw
Managing Editor: Bridget Giles
Art Director: Dave Goodman

Gareth Stevens Editor: Betsy Rasmussen
Gareth Stevens Designer: Melissa Valuch

Picture Credits: Cover: The Rio Grande Gorge. (Skyscan: Jim Wark)
Contents: The Rio Grande passes through Big Bend National Park, Texas.

Key: l–left, r–right, t–top, b–bottom, c–center.
Ardea: John Cancalosi 10; Bat Conservation International, www.batcon.org: Merlin D. Tuttle 12t; Corbis:
29t; Tom Bean 8/9; Steve Bein 4; Franz-Marc Frei 15; Annie Griffiths Belt 26; Liz Hymans 28; Buddy Mays
11, 24; Mark Rykoff 21; Lee Snider 14; Adam Woolfitt 18; Getty Images: 16; Library of Congress: 20;
NASA: 8b; NHPA: 12c; Peter Newark's Pictures: 17; PhotoDisc: Scenics of America 22; Jeremy
Woodhouse 7; Still Pictures: Peter Arnold/Lionel Atwill 12b; Peter Arnold/Los Alamos National
Laboratories 23; Sylvia Cordaiy Picture Library: Anthony Bloomfield 5t; Topham: Bob Daemmrich 13;
Jack Kurtz 5b; Travel Ink: Ronald Badkin 29b; David Forman 9b, 27; Barry Hughes 19; U.S. Customs
Service: James R. Tourtellotte 25t, 25b

Printed in the United States of America

1 2 3 4 5 6 7 8 9 07 06 05 04 03

Table of Contents

The Big River

The Rio Grande is an important river. It flows through an area that is almost a desert, and the river's water is valuable to farmers and city residents along the river.

Above: *The Rio Grande flows through Santa Elena Canyon in the Big Bend region of Texas.*

*R*io Grande means "big river" in Spanish. This name is deserved because the Rio Grande is the third-longest river in the United States and the twenty-fourth longest in the world. Although it is nearly 2,000 miles (3,200 kilometers) long, however, the Rio Grande is shallow and does not contain a lot of water throughout much of its length. This is because most of the river flows through some of the driest regions in North America, and because its water is used by so many people.

The Rio Grande's limited amount of water is vitally important for the people and wildlife that live in the river's basin.

Water Course

The Rio Grande begins high in the San Juan Mountains of southern Colorado. It flows south through New Mexico and along the border between Texas and Mexico before

Right: *Taos Pueblo near the Rio Grande in New Mexico. Villages like these have been built by Native people for hundreds of years.*

it empties into the Gulf of Mexico near Brownsville, Texas.

In Mexico, the river is known as the *Río Bravo del Norte*, which means "bold river of the north."

Lifeline

On its journey south, the river flows down from the mountains and across plateaus before reaching the dry land of southern New Mexico, Texas, and northern Mexico. In these hot, dry areas, the Rio Grande is too shallow for large cargo ships or barges to travel on. It is, however, a source of water for farms and has been used for irrigation for more than two thousand years.

In the last century, several dams were built on the Rio Grande to create reservoirs and to generate hydroelectric power. Many cities in the area are supplied with river water collected behind these dams. Thanks to these supplies of water, the cities have grown in size rapidly in recent years as companies and people move to the area.

Today, the dams store so much water from the river that water levels farther downstream become very low. By the time the river reaches the ocean, it is little more than a stream.

A sign on a bridge over the Rio Grande in El Paso, Texas, marks the U.S. and Mexico border.

1 From Source to Mouth

While most other rivers collect more and more water as they approach the ocean, the Rio Grande actually loses water. In summer, only a trickle of water gets as far as the river's mouth.

The Rio Grande begins in the San Juan Mountains in southern Colorado. The source of the river is 12,000 feet (3,660 meters) above sea level. Most of the river's water comes from melting snow, but it is also fed by underground springs. The river's basin is one of the largest in the world at 336,000 square miles (870,250 sq km), but because much of the region is so dry, nearly all the river's water comes from just half of this large area.

The Shrinking River

The river is 1,885 miles (3,030 km) long and flows south through New Mexico and then southeast along the Texas and Mexico border before it empties into the Gulf of Mexico between Brownsville, Texas, and Matamoros, Mexico.

The Rio Grande actually loses water as it flows to the sea. The river's irrigation projects do take water from

KEY FACTS	
Length:	1,885 miles (3,030 km)
Drainage basin:	336,000 square miles (870,250 sq km)
Source:	San Juan Mountains, Colorado
Mouth:	Gulf of Mexico
Other features:	Rio Grande Gorge, NM; Big Bend, TX
Economic uses:	Irrigation, hydroelectric power, water for cities
Major dams:	Elephant Butte Dam, Amistad Dam, Falcon Dam
Major cities:	Albuquerque, NM; El Paso, Laredo, and Brownsville, TX; Ciudad Juarez, Nuevo Laredo, and Matamoros, Mexico

the river, but the river shrinks naturally anyway. The heat from the sun evaporates some of the water, and more seeps out into its sandy banks. The river is shallowest near its mouth, especially in years when there has not been a heavy fall of snow in the mountains upstream.

Three Sections

When people talk about the Rio Grande, they sometimes divide it into three sections:

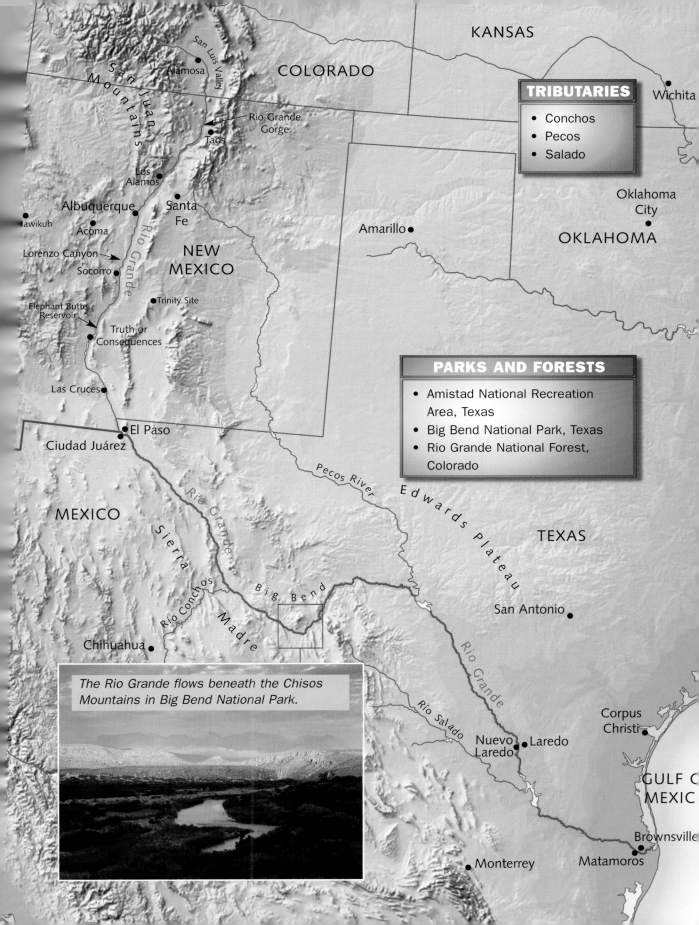

KANSAS

COLORADO

San Juan Mountains

San Luis Valley

Alamosa

Rio Grande Gorge

Taos

Los Alamos

Albuquerque

Santa Fe

awikuh

Acoma

Lorenzo Canyon

Socorro

Elephant Butte Reservoir

Truth or Consequences

Las Cruces

El Paso

Ciudad Juárez

MEXICO

Sierra

Rio Conchos

Chihuahua

Rio Grande

Madre

Big Bend

NEW MEXICO

Trinity Site

Amarillo

Wichita

Oklahoma City

OKLAHOMA

Pecos River

Edwards Plateau

TEXAS

San Antonio

Rio Grande

Rio Salado

Nuevo Laredo

Laredo

Corpus Christi

GULF O MEXIC

Brownsville

Matamoros

Monterrey

TRIBUTARIES

- Conchos
- Pecos
- Salado

PARKS AND FORESTS

- Amistad National Recreation Area, Texas
- Big Bend National Park, Texas
- Rio Grande National Forest, Colorado

The Rio Grande flows beneath the Chisos Mountains in Big Bend National Park.

upper, middle, and lower. The upper section starts at the river's source. It extends down through the valleys of Colorado and northern New Mexico, where it is fed by numerous streams. It also flows over a dry plateau south of Albuquerque, New Mexico.

Into the Desert

The middle section of the Rio Grande begins as the river flows between the cities of El Paso, Texas, and Ciudad Juarez, Mexico. The river runs southeast until it is joined by the Río Conchos, its largest tributary, which flows down from mountains in Mexico. Downstream from this point, the river takes a change of course and skirts around the Sierra Madre mountains at a place called Big Bend.

The river then turns east and is joined from the north by another important tributary, the Pecos River. The Rio Grande swings around to the southeast again and flows along the edge of a high plateau that spreads north into central Texas. This area is the driest part of the river's course.

The lower section of the

river begins where it widens downstream from Laredo, Texas. The Rio Grande is then joined by the Río Salado, another tributary, before continuing to its mouth a few miles downstream from Brownsville. To help control the supply of water, dams have been built across the middle and lower river. The dams create large reservoirs behind them.

Beauty Spots

The Rio Grande has several famous natural wonders along its length, including canyons, hot springs, and lakes. On the upper river at Taos, New Mexico, the river has formed the Rio Grande Gorge. The gorge is 37 miles

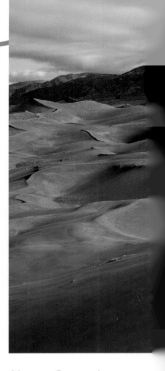

Above: *Dunes in the San Luis Valley, Colorado. The dunes are formed by wind blowing down the river valley.*

Right: *The mouth of the river as seen from space. The river forms a network of channels, dunes, and lagoons.*

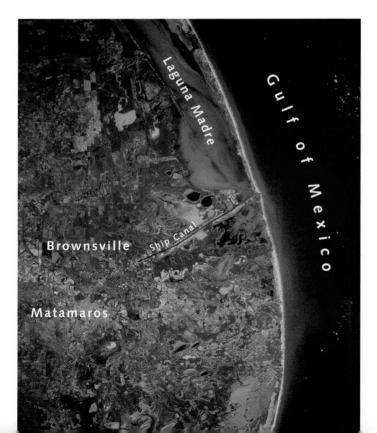

Laguna Madre

Gulf of Mexico

Ship Canal

Brownsville

Matamaros

(60 km) long and 800 feet (243 m) deep. The river has also formed San Lorenzo Canyon, a few miles north of Socorro, New Mexico.

Probably the most famous section of the river is the mountainous Big Bend region in Texas, which is protected as a national park. Here the river flows through rugged mountains and cuts three deep canyons. Seashell and dinosaur fossils have been found in rocks in areas of the park.

The lower section of the Rio Grande is famous for its unusual lakes, known locally as resacas. Resacas are similar to oxbow lakes— they are created when the wide river floods into low-lying areas along the banks. When the floodwaters recede, marshy lakes are

Below: *The Rio Grande Gorge near Taos, New Mexico, formed by the river cutting through volcanic rocks.*

left behind. Later, when the river floods again from heavy rains upstream, the resacas are refilled. Many animals, especially birds, rely on the resacas, living among the rushes that grow on their banks and in the shallow water. Many Native communities also used the water from resacas to irrigate their crops.

Over the years, the river's course has changed direction, and resacas are no longer filled by regular flooding. In other cases, dams have stopped floodwater from reaching them. These resacas now rely on occasional rain to refill them, and many are dry for much of the year.

2 The Life of the River

Dams and pollution have had a severe effect on the Rio Grande's fragile environment. However, a variety of interesting plants and animals still manage to survive here.

Above: *A greater roadrunner dashes along the ground. Roadrunners are speedy birds that often run along roads in front of vehicles.*

The San Juan Mountains of Colorado, where the Rio Grande begins, receive more rain and snow than any other part of the river. As the river descends through New Mexico, the climate becomes hotter and drier. Summer storms bring heavy rainfall to parts of the upper river every year, and the hills in the north of New Mexico are often covered with snow in winter. While the lower section of the river is often hit by fierce storms coming in from the Gulf of Mexico, the climate around the middle section of the river is hot and dry for most of the year.

Wild World

A wide range of plant and animal life can be found along the river's course because it passes through environments that differ greatly.

Both deciduous and evergreen trees grow in the river's mountainous regions, and bald and golden eagles and black bears are just some of the animals living there. As the river descends to the hotter and drier plateau in southern New Mexico and Texas, water-efficient plants, such as creosote bushes, ocotillo, and agave, grow.

The animals living on the plateau include coyotes, wild cats, mule deer, peregrine falcons, and roadrunners, as well as several rattlesnake

TRAPPED FISH

Nearly half of the Rio Grande's fish species have died out in the last one hundred years. This is due to pollution from farms and cities and changes in the river caused by dams and irrigation.

The Rio Grande silvery minnow is a good example of an endangered species. The silvery minnow is a fish about 3.5 inches (9 centimeters) long, with scales that give off a greenish reflection. They were once common in all parts of the Rio Grande, but today, silvery minnows only survive in a 170-mile (272-km) stretch of the river in New Mexico, between Cochiti Dam (west of Santa Fe) and Elephant Butte Dam (near Truth or Consequences).

The silvery minnow's eggs float downstream and hatch far from where they were laid. Many of the eggs and young fish end up in irrigation canals, where they die. Fish hatched from eggs that have washed through a dam cannot swim back up the river to breed, and so the silvery minnows remain trapped between the two dams.

species, many types of lizards, and tarantula spiders. The collared peccary, a piglike animal that is native to the United States, is also found in this area. Peccaries look like small boars, and they generally travel together in groups of about twelve. Peccaries feed on agave cacti, prickly pears, roots, and insect larvae. They also damage crops, and farmers sometimes shoot peccaries to keep them off of farmland.

Above: *Elephant Butte Reservoir is one of the few places where Rio Grande silvery minnows survive.*

Southern Visitors

Mexican long-nosed bats are sometimes seen around the lower section of the Rio Grande. This rare type of bat feeds on nectar and pollen from plants such as agave cacti. The long-nosed bats pollinate agave cacti by transferring pollen between plants as they feed. The bats search for food over large areas, traveling as far north as the Big Bend.

Mexican black bears also live in the north region. Although they are native to the lower section of the river, many moved into Big Bend National Park after the area's native bears were wiped out by hunters.

Dry Forest

An unusual type of forest grows along parts of the middle and lower river. The forest is called a bosque, and it contains cottonwood

Right: *A long-nosed bat uses its long, pink tongue to lick up food, and yellow pollen sticks to its face.*

Right: *An agave cactus in full bloom. Without bats pollinating them, these plants would not be able to produce seeds.*

Below: *A female collared peccary and her young search for food. These animals are related to pigs.*

RIVER DAMAGE

Even though they prevent devastating floods and make life easier for the people living in the river's cities, dams have harmed the Rio Grande's wildlife and fragile natural features. The dams divert water onto fields to water crops, so less water gets to the lower sections of the river. The banks of the river are drying out in some places and falling away (below). Without regular floods, many of the river's resacas are staying dry for years at a time, driving wildlife away.

Irrigation is also a problem. Without it, crops of food could not grow, but irrigation can eventually damage the soil by washing away all the nutrients needed by plants and leaving dried salts behind. Farmers then must add more chemicals to the soil to nourish it. A lot of these chemicals get washed into the river, adding to pollution.

People are trying to solve these problems by using irrigation water more efficiently. Water is also being released from reservoirs more often so lower areas do not get too dry.

and willow trees. Birds, such as ducks, geese, and cranes, migrating north in summer stop to rest in bosques.

The trees in bosques thrive best after the river floods. The Rio Grande used to flood every few years. However, most of the Rio Grande's areas of bosque have been destroyed by the creation of flood controls along the river.

Non-native salt cedar and Russian olive trees have taken over the area's natural bosque. Forests of these new trees soak up more water than bosque plants and make the ground even drier than before. Conservation groups are working to restore bosque areas by replanting native trees and allowing water to flood into the forests regularly.

3 River of Villages

The Puebloan people have built their adobe houses beside the Rio Grande for hundreds of years. These settlements are the oldest towns in the United States.

People have probably been living along the Rio Grande for at least ten thousand years. In the earliest days, Native people survived by hunting deer and birds that lived in the area. It was a hard life because only a few animals could survive in the dry lands of the river's basin.

About three thousand years ago, Native people called the Chichimecs moved to the area from Mexico. They learned to use water from rivers to farm crops such as corn, beans, and squashes. They no longer needed to rely on hunting for their food.

The First Towns

The Chichimecs built small towns near their farms. These villages were built mainly from stone or adobe —a type of brick made from clay and straw that is dried in the Sun. The buildings

Below: *The Puye Cliff Dwellings in New Mexico, a few miles west of the Rio Grande. The dwellings were inhabited by Anasazi people for nearly one thousand years, until 1580.*

were constructed around central plazas. The villages were generally peaceful communities.

This way of life is now known as the Anasazi tradition. (*Anasazi* means "the ancient ones" in the Navajo language). The Anasazi settlers along the Rio Grande used the river for irrigation, and their farms prospered even in times of drought.

The descendants of the Anasazi culture are known as the Puebloans. *Pueblo* means "village" in Spanish, and the Rio Grande's Native settlements are still called by that name. The Puebloan people lived in farming communities just like their ancestors, but they built larger and stronger houses, grew more crops, made more sophisticated pottery, and wove cloth from cotton.

Shipwrecked Explorers

In the 1530s, less than forty years after Columbus's voyage to the Americas, a small band of European explorers shipwrecked off the coast of what is now Texas. They traveled inland and visited several pueblos near the Rio Grande. One of these men was Estevanico, a Moroccan slave, who was probably the first African to reach North America.

PUEBLO WATERWORKS

Irrigation was essential for the Native people who lived near the Rio Grande. The Puebloan people supplied water to their crops through a system of ditches that crisscrossed their fields like a checkerboard. These ditches branched off from a central canal leading from the river. Water was diverted into this canal by small dams. The dams were made of logs and brush and extended into the river but did not block it completely. All of the canals had to be dug using wooden hoes and stone axes. Some canals were built to carry water into the pueblos themselves. Farmers in the region still use a similar system of ditches, called acequias, to water their fields.

Above: *Water is carried across a ditch by a hollowed log. Simple irrigation technology has been used in the Rio Grande area for hundreds of years.*

Above: *Coronado and his large expedition of Spanish soldiers and Native guides. His men were the first people to record seeing the Grand Canyon and the Painted Desert.*

In 1536, after living for years with Native people in the Rio Grande area, Estevanico and the other survivors traveled to New Spain—the Spanish colony in what is now Mexico.

Visions of Gold

In 1539, the Spanish decided to explore the unknown land to the north, and Estevanico agreed to guide the party. Estevanico came upon the Hawikuh Pueblo, about 100 miles (160 km) west of the Rio Grande. From a distance, the straw in the adobe bricks sparkled in the Sun, and the explorers mistook it for gold. Estevanico was later killed by the Hawikuh people, and his companions fled back to New Spain.

In New Spain, those that survived said they had seen seven cities made of gold, and Hawikuh came to be called the Seven Cities of Cibola. Francisco Vasquez de

THE PUEBLO REVOLT

Between 1598 and 1680, the Puebloan people were ruled by the Spanish. The Spanish treated the Native people cruelly and forced them to live like Europeans. They killed Puebloans for worshipping their own gods and carrying out religious rituals.

In 1680, the Puebloans united to force the Spanish out. Their leader was a man called Pope (pronounced po-pay). Pope coordinated the uprising by using runners to relay plans between villages. This was difficult because the uprising involved about seventy pueblos, and some were as far as 300 miles (480 km) apart. The uprising was successful, and the Puebloan people lived freely for twelve years, until the Spanish conquered them again in 1692.

Coronado, another Spanish explorer, took an army to Hawikuh in 1540 and defeated the Puebloan people in the first major battle to take place in North America between Europeans and Natives.

The Spaniards soon found that the pueblos were made of clay, not gold, and they headed for the Rio Grande looking for other treasures. They spent the winter in Tiguex, a riverside pueblo where Bernalillo, New Mexico, a town close to Albuquerque, is today. During the winter, Coronado's men fought several battles with the Puebloans. Coronado kept Tiguex as his base and spent 1541 exploring as far away as Kansas before returning empty-handed to Spain.

Spanish Rule

In 1598, Spanish general Juan de Onate crossed the Rio Grande, claiming the area beyond for Spain.

Above: *A scene from the 1680 Pueblo Revolt, when Native fighters overwhelmed Spanish rulers.*

Acoma Pueblo in New Mexico is still lived in by Native people and has been inhabited for nearly one thousand years. This makes it the longest-inhabited town in North America.

He named the crossing point *El Paso del Río Del Norte*—"ford of the river of the north." The name stuck, and when Spanish priests built a mission there in 1659, they named it El Paso. The Texan city of that name stands in the same place today.

Onate also named the new Spanish territory New Mexico, although it also contained parts of what is now Texas and Arizona. Farther up the river, Onate came upon a Pueblo village in the hills and built a settlement there, which became the present-day city of Santa Fe, New Mexico.

Sky City

In 1599, Onate defeated the Acoma Pueblo 50 miles (80 km) west of the Rio Grande. Acoma Pueblo—also called Sky City—is built on top of a mesa (a steep, flat-topped hill). Despite holding out for a time, the Native warriors could not defend their home against Spanish cannons.

Onate's army took control, and the Spanish soon ruled over all the Pueblo peoples in the Rio Grande area. Santa Fe became the capital of New Mexico in 1610. (The city remained the capital when New Mexico became a U.S. state, making it the oldest state capital in the country.)

T OR C

One town beside the Rio Grande in New Mexico earned its name in a very unusual way. Truth or Consequences, New Mexico, often called T or C, was originally named Palomas Springs. The town is known for its natural springs, which were used by Native people for hundreds of years before the town was built there in 1910. In 1914, Palomas Springs changed its name to Hot Springs, in an attempt to attract more residents and visitors. In 1950, Ralph Edwards, the host of the nationwide radio show *Truth or Consequences*, offered to broadcast every year from any city that was willing to change its name to Truth or Consequences. The people of Hot Springs saw their chance to put their hometown on the map and voted to change the town's name. The following year, Ralph Edwards broadcast live from Truth or Consequences, New Mexico. Every year since then, the people of Truth or Consequences celebrate their history at the Ralph Edward's Fiesta.

In 1680, the Pueblo people rebelled and forced the Spanish out. The Spanish soon took control again, however, and as more settlers arrived, they founded Albuquerque beside the Rio Grande in 1706. When Mexico became independent from Spain in 1821, the Rio Grande became a part of Mexico's property as well.

U.S. Settlers

In the early years of the nineteenth century, settlers from the United States began arriving in Mexican-ruled Texas. In 1835, the people of Texas rebelled against the Mexican government. After the Texas Revolution, which

THE TREATY OF GUADALUPE HIDALGO

The Mexican War ended when the United States and Mexico signed the Treaty of Guadalupe Hidalgo in 1848. The treaty established the Rio Grande as the border between Mexico and the United States and gave the United States over 500,000 square miles (1,295,000 sq km) of Mexican land—almost half Mexico's territory. This land became California, Nevada, Utah, and parts of Colorado, Arizona, New Mexico and Wyoming. Mexico also gave up all claims to Texas. In return, the United States paid Mexico fifteen million dollars.

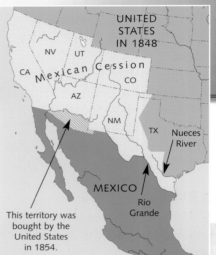

Below: *The Battle of Palo Alto, the first battle in the Mexican War.*

This territory was bought by the United States in 1854.

included the famous battle at the Alamo, Texas became a separate country, bordering Mexico along the Nueces River, about 120 miles (192 km) north of the Rio Grande.

In 1845, Texas became a U.S. state, although Mexico still claimed the area belonged to them. The Mexican War (1846–1848) broke out as the two countries fought over land throughout the Southwest. When the United States won the war, the Mexicans agreed, among other things, to hand over New Mexico and to make the Rio Grande the new border with Texas.

To Modern Times
After the Mexican War, more U.S. settlers arrived in the Rio Grande area. Groups often argued about their limited supplies of water from the river.

By the early twentieth century, the Rio Grande was still a quiet river, with only a small number of people living beside it. The river's shallowness prevented it from being used to bring products in or out of the area, and much of the land was too dry for farming.

After World War II (1939–1945), manufacturing industries came to the area, and new farming and irrigation techniques made agriculture easier. Because of this, the river's cities, especially those in Mexico, have grown rapidly in the last fifty years.

Below: *A picture postcard from 1908 showing International Bridge over the Rio Grande from El Paso to Ciudad Juarez.*

4 A Vital Source

The Rio Grande's water is stretched to the limit to supply farms and cities, and the cities along the U.S. and Mexico border are home to some of the poorest people in North America.

The Rio Grande Basin has a rapidly growing population, which is putting huge demands on the river's limited water supplies.

People move to cities along the river looking for jobs. Each city has different types of jobs that are available. Agriculture is the only major industry that employs people along the river's entire course.

Building Houses

It is easiest to find a job in the upper Rio Grande region. All new arrivals to the area need a place to live, and homebuilding is big business in that region, including in the San Luis

Above:
Albuquerque is the largest city in New Mexico and one of the largest on the Rio Grande.

THE FIRST NUCLEAR WEAPONS

In 1943, during World War II, a group of nuclear scientists began the Manhattan Project in a laboratory at Los Alamos, a few miles west of the Rio Grande in northern New Mexico. The scientists were working in secret for the U.S. military, inventing the first nuclear weapons.

Two years later, on July 16, 1945, the world's first nuclear bomb was detonated at Trinity Site near the Oscura Mountains about 30 miles (48 km) east of the Rio Grande's Elephant Butte Lake in central New Mexico.

A few weeks later, other bombs developed at Los Alamos were dropped on the cities of Hiroshima and Nagasaki in Japan, with whom the United States was at war. Japan surrendered after the bombs killed and injured hundreds of thousands of Japanese civilians. Today, the Los Alamos National Laboratory is still an important center of nuclear research. Other weapon technologies, such as missile guidance systems, are developed nearby in the Sandia National Laboratories in Albuquerque.

In 1945, the world's first nuclear bomb is exploded in the desert a few miles from the Rio Grande.

Valley and near the city of Santa Fe.

Agriculture is the main industry along the upper river, where high rainfall and melting snow means farmers do not have to rely as much on irrigation water. The crops grown here include potatoes, lettuce, spinach, carrots, and alfalfa (a leafy plant fed to cattle).

Some of the area's water comes from underground springs, so farms and cities are not overly dependent on the river. The people who take water from the upper Rio Grande must leave a certain amount of water in the river to flow down to the drier lands beyond.

Water Needed

Irrigation is more important to the people in the middle and lower regions of the river, where the climate is much drier. In the early parts of the twentieth century, the Rio Grande Project dammed the river in several places between northern New Mexico and southern Texas. The largest dam there is Elephant Butte Dam near Truth or Consequences, New Mexico. Many of the river's dams generate electricity, but their main role is to store valuable water and to control floods.

More than 1,000 miles (1,600 km) of irrigation canals supply dammed water to farmland in Texas, New Mexico, and Mexico.

Groundwater is crucial for supplying extra water, but so much has been pumped from underground that the land is beginning to sink.

Crops grown along the middle river include cotton and grain, while citrus fruits and sugarcane are grown on the lower river.

Growing Cities

Large numbers of people are moving into the region's

Above: *The Elephant Butte Dam has created a large reservoir that is popular with water sports enthusiasts.*

Above right: *A drug smuggler is arrested by Border Patrol officers.*

Right: *Law agents patrol remote areas looking for evidence of illegal activity.*

BORDER CONTROLS ALONG THE RIO GRANDE

Illegal immigration from Mexico to the United States across the Rio Grande has increased greatly in the last twenty years, as unemployed people from Mexico and other Central American countries travel to the United States in search of work. Smugglers also carry drugs across the river to sell in the United States.

The U.S. Border Patrol exists to stop people crossing into the United States illegally. The border guards use long-range night-vision scopes and heat and movement sensors, as well as searchlights and tracking methods to locate people coming across the river. They also patrol the more remote desert regions in all-terrain vehicles, in helicopters, and even on horses. Places where the river is especially narrow or shallow are blocked with several fences to make it harder for illegal immigrants to cross.

Illegal immigrants sometimes choose to cross through very remote and unprotected areas of the border. This is risky and about 370 people die crossing the border every year.

cities on both the U.S. and Mexico sides of the river. This is partly because the river's farming industry has been damaged by pollution, lack of available water, or even too much irrigation. In hot areas, irrigation water evaporates, leaving salt in the soil and making it impossible to grow

Above: *Mexican workers assemble electronic equipment in one of hundreds of factories on the U.S. and Mexico border.*

anything. Many farm owners, especially those in the dry parts of Mexico, have had to let go some of their workers, who then move to Ciudad Juarez, Nuevo Laredo, and other cities to work.

In the Mexican cities, jobs are available in the many maquiladoras. These are assembly plants, and they are owned mainly by non-Mexican companies. These companies pay Mexican employees lower wages than U.S. factory employees earn, but it is more than people are paid elsewhere in Mexico. Everything from electrical goods and automobile parts to jeans are made in maquiladoras. Maquiladoras are sometimes called "twin plants," because components are sent from the U.S. side of the river to the Mexican side to be assembled.

Many jobless Mexicans and people from other Central American countries make their way to the Rio Grande in hopes of crossing it, either legally or illegally, and finding work in the United States. Most of these new arrivals end up living in shanty towns, known as colonias, which do not have proper sewers or supplies of clean water.

Lack of Resources

The crowded cities of the Rio Grande need more water and electricity. If Rio Grande dams hold back water to make electricity, less water reaches farms and cities downstream, so many cities take water from other sources, such as wells. Some cities, including El Paso, Texas, and Las Cruces, New Mexico, save water by recycling irrigation water and supplying it to houses and businesses. Because the Rio Grande is too shallow for commercial navigation, it is not used to transport people or cargo. Instead, railroads and highways have to be used to transport goods, causing more pollution and making transportation in the area expensive.

THE RIO GRANDE BASIN COALITION

The Rio Grande Basin Coalition is a collection of conservation groups that help protect the river's environment and improve the life of local people. The coalition was set up in 1994 and now includes more than fifty organizations from both the United States and Mexico. Every year since 1995, the coalition has sponsored Dia del Río (River Day), during which volunteers from all along the Rio Grande plant native trees, cleanup the riverbanks, and hold events to raise money and teach people about the importance of conserving the river.

The coalition also trains local people so they can get jobs in the region, and it works with managers of the maquiladoras (factories) to improve conditions for the many people who work in them.

Among other things, the Rio Grande Coalition is working to preserve natural river forests, or bosque.

5 Places to Visit

From deep gorges and ancient Native dwellings to battlefields and wilderness areas, there is a lot to see along the Rio Grande.

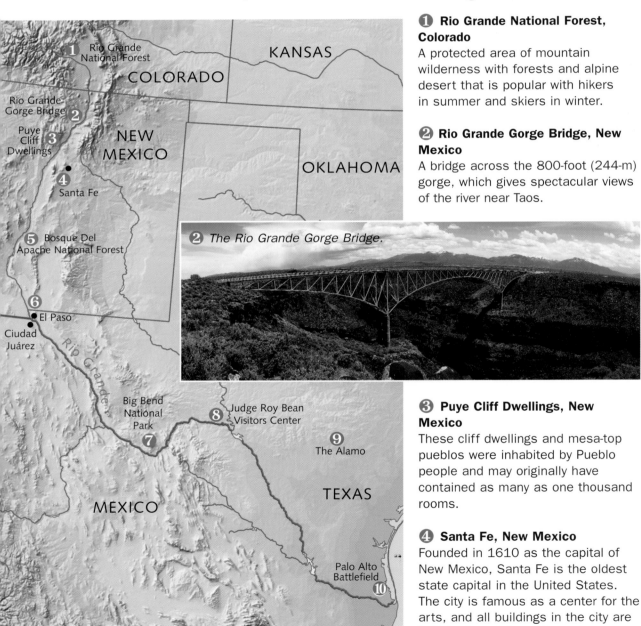

1 The Rio Grande Gorge Bridge.

❶ Rio Grande National Forest, Colorado
A protected area of mountain wilderness with forests and alpine desert that is popular with hikers in summer and skiers in winter.

❷ Rio Grande Gorge Bridge, New Mexico
A bridge across the 800-foot (244-m) gorge, which gives spectacular views of the river near Taos.

❸ Puye Cliff Dwellings, New Mexico
These cliff dwellings and mesa-top pueblos were inhabited by Pueblo people and may originally have contained as many as one thousand rooms.

❹ Santa Fe, New Mexico
Founded in 1610 as the capital of New Mexico, Santa Fe is the oldest state capital in the United States. The city is famous as a center for the arts, and all buildings in the city are built in the adobe style.

⑤ Bosque Del Apache National Forest, New Mexico

A protected area containing a resaca surrounded by woodland unique to the Rio Grande area.

⑥ Ciudad Juarez, Mexico, and El Paso, Texas

The largest cities on the Rio Grande are home to more than one million people and linked by a bridge. The border between the two cities was disputed for nearly one hundred years. In 1864, the Rio Grande changed course leaving some Mexican land on the U.S. side. The dispute was finally settled in 1963.

⑦ Big Bend National Park, Texas

The largest national park along the Rio Grande. The park contains spectacular canyons, fossils of trees and dinosaurs, and the remains of ancient cave dwellings.

⑧ Judge Roy Bean Visitors Center, Texas

Judge Roy Bean was a saloonkeeper and justice of the peace, where the Pecos and Rio Grande rivers meet.

Judge Bean held his court at the bar inside his saloon (below). He became famous for his odd rulings and boasted that he was the "law west of the Pecos."

Above: *Judge Roy Bean's saloon.*

⑨ The Alamo, Texas

The site of a thirteen-day siege during the Texas Revolution in 1836. More than 150 Texans, including the famous frontiersmen James Bowie and Davy Crockett, held off Mexican soldiers before being overrun and killed.

⑩ Palo Alto Battlefield Historic Site, Texas

The first battle of the Mexican War took place here in May 1846, when General Zachary Taylor crossed the Rio Grande to take the city of Matamoros.

⑨ *The ruined Alamo mission still stands in the center of San Antonio.*

How Rivers Form

Rivers have many features that are constantly changing in shape. The illustration below shows how these features are created.

Rivers flow from mountains to oceans, receiving water from rain, melting snow, and underground springs. Rivers collect their water from an area called the river basin. High mountain ridges form the divides between river basins.

Tributaries join the main river at places called confluences. Rivers flow down steep mountain slopes quickly but slow as they near the ocean and gather more water. Slow rivers have many meanders (wide turns) and often change course.

Near the mouth, levees (piles of mud) build up on the banks. The levees stop water from draining into the river, creating areas of swamp.

❶ **Glacier:** An ice mass that melts into river water.

❷ **Lake:** The source of many rivers; may be fed by springs or precipitation.

❸ **Rapids:** Shallow water that flows quickly.

❹ **Waterfall:** Formed when a river wears away softer rock, making a step in the riverbed.

❺ **Canyon:** Formed when a river cuts a channel through rock.

❻ **Floodplain:** A place where rivers often flood flat areas, depositing mud.

❼ **Oxbow lake:** River bend cut off when a river changes course, leaving water behind.

❽ **Estuary:** River mouth where river and ocean water mix together.

❾ **Delta:** Triangular river mouth created when mud islands form, splitting the flow into several channels called distributaries.

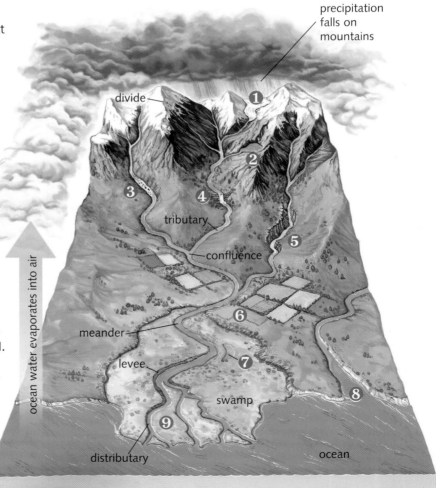

precipitation falls on mountains

divide

tributary

confluence

ocean water evaporates into air

meander

levee

swamp

distributary

ocean

Glossary

agriculture The practice of growing crops and raising livestock as an industry.

basin The area drained by a river and its tributaries.

cargo Transported products or merchandise.

confluence The place where rivers meet.

conservation Protection of natural resources and the environment.

dam A a constructed barrier across a river that controls the flow of water.

drought Continuous dry weather.

evaporate When a liquid, such as water, turns into a vapor or gas.

gorge A narrow, steep-sided valley or canyon.

immigrant A person who moves to another country from his or her native land.

industry Producing things or providing services in order to earn money.

irrigation Watering crops with water from a river, lake, or other source.

migration A regular journey undertaken by a group of animals from one climate to another for feeding and breeding purposes.

navigate To travel through water, steering in an attempt to avoid obstacles.

reservoir An artificial lake where water is stored for later use.

source The place where a river begins.

terrain The features of an area of land.

tributary A river that flows into a larger river at a confluence.

valley A hollow channel cut by a river, usually between ranges of hills or mountains.

For Further Information

Books

Cordva, Amy. *My Land Sings: Stories from the Rio Grande.* HarperTrophy, 2001.

Crewe, Sabrina. *The Anasazi Culture at Mesa Verde.* Gareth Stevens, 2003.

Lourie, Peter. *Rio Grande: From the Rocky Mountains to the Gulf of Mexico.* Boyds Mills Press, 2000.

Parker, Steve. *Eyewitness: Pond and River.* DK Publishing, 2000.

Web Sites

Big Bend National Park
www.nps.gov/bibe/

The Friends Rio Grande Nature Center
www.frgnc.org

Indian Pueblo Cultural Center
www.indianpueblo.org/ipcc

Rio Grande/Río Bravo Basin Coalition
www.rioweb.org

Index